HIRAETH

Moonlight *Shadows* Whispering *Melancholy*

Shadows that whisper,
hearts that mourn

VARDAAN VIKRAM SINGH

INDIA • SINGAPORE • MALAYSIA

ISBN
Paperback 979-8-89588-616-8
Hardcase 979-8-89632-997-8

Dedication

With emotions swirling like a macrocosmic tide and memories and love cascading through every chamber of my heart, I dedicate my debut poetry collection to:

My paternal grandparents, whose love and legacy continue to inspire me:

Late Shri Baburam
Late Smt. Savitri Devi

And to my maternal grandparents, whose guidance and wisdom have shaped me:

Shri Narendra Singh Bishnoi
Smt. Ved Prabha Bishnoi

May their love, wisdom, and memories forever resonate within these pages.

Contents

Eclipse

Elysium

Saudade

Acknowledgement

As I embark on this literary journey, I am filled with gratitude for the love, guidance, and support that has shaped me into the person I am today.

First and foremost, I extend my deepest gratitude to:

My dearest Melancholy, my bosom friend Yearning, and my ever-so-friendly Fate. Your relentless presence has gushed within me, a calming grief that flows in the words of this book.

To the individuals and I have met and lost, my former friends with their lavish ways to doubt my abilities and talk behind my back, enjoy the irony! Those who betrayed me, for those to whom I was a honey box and colleagues who spilled their hatred on me, your actions have been nothing more than a catalyst to my poetry.

Family

To my mother, Dr. Abha Singh, whose teachings and guidance have been my guiding light, I thank you for instilling in me the love for words and the courage to express myself. Your unwavering faith in me has been my greatest strength.

To my father, Dr. Vikram Singh, a celebrated poet and author, I thank you for being my inspiration, mentor, and constant source of encouragement. Your love for literature has been contagious, and I am forever grateful for the gift of language you have passed on to me.

To my sisters, Stuti and Avidha , my brother-in-law, Abhishek ji and my dearest six-month-old nephew, Rudra, whose gurgles and giggles make up the best part of my day and my entire family, I thank you for your unconditional love, support, and patience. Your presence in my life has made this journey worthwhile.

Teachers

To Ma'am Sunita Nayar, Ma'am Anita Sahai and the beloved Ma'am Mala, whose memory lives on in these pages. Your guidance was the lighthouse that illuminated my path, nurturing the inner poet within me. Your unwavering encouragement and kindness unearthed my writing potential. Your mentorship was the fire that ignited my creative flame, and your compassion the wind that fanned it into fire.

To Ma'am Shreshtha Bhadoria, I thank you for your meticulous proofreading and valuable guidance. Your expertise has refined my work, and I am deeply grateful.

Friends

To Samya and Sonam, my dear friends and confidants, I extend my heartfelt gratitude for your priceless contributions to this book.
From design to layout, themes, and illustrations, your creative input has brought this collection to life. Your selflessness and enthusiasm have been invaluable.

To Isam, Sudhanshu and Abhinab, its been one of my very pleasures to have found a guiding and caring brothers in the form of you. Your designing expertise has brought light and a new form to this book. Your welcoming spirit and hospitable nature has been one of the greatest presents, this book has received.

To Achintya, your constant support and encouragement have been a source of strength throughout this journey. Thank you for being a pillar of support.

This collection would not have been possible without the collective efforts of these remarkable individuals. I am humbled by their love, trust, and faith in me.

In embracing the darkness, I have indeed found light. Thank you.

Introduction

In the depths of my own longing, Hiraeth gleamed
before me. As I steered through the moonlit
shores of love, loss and memory, I found solace in the
gushing words that vein out of my grief onto the pages of
this book.

Rising from the ashes of the lost, burning in the flames
of melancholy, 'Hiraeth' emerges as a flicker of fire,
casting shadows of longing.
A yearning for atonement, or a mourning for the
forgotten? A lingering homesickness for the smiles that
departed and the giggles we now lament.

Join me on this hitchhiker's voyage, where the Journey
itself becomes the destination. With each poem, I
invite each passerby to navigate through the angels
and demons of my soul, exploring the intersections of
affection and Saudade.

Foreword

The collection of poems on different issues of life, which a growing child experiences, has been given a very interesting and meaningful name: Hiraeth. This term is used in the context of homesickness tinged with grief and an awareness of the presence of absence. It evokes a feeling in which pain and joy are braided so tightly that they cannot be untangled. This concept, deeply interwoven into the Welsh psyche, is felt on a national level and carries the profound sense of longing and loss. It is the homesickness for a place, a personal yearning for the soul to miss something beloved. It is a longing for a home to which one cannot return, or perhaps for a house that may never have existed.

The collection of poems entitled Hiraeth by Vardaan Vikram Singh is a commendable expression of an adolescent reflecting on completing about 18 years with an ancestral family-a time filled with love, affection, and invaluable lessons for the journey ahead. This departure from childhood brings with it the bittersweet realization that the best part of life is coming to a close. These emotions, intertwined with the bonds of relationships and a deep attachment to the land, find their way into heartfelt expressions on paper. Such expressions create something memorable, preserved within the covers of this collection of poems.

This collection reflects different moods across various phases and occasions.

The writer is gracious in expressing gratitude to family members, close relations, and friends. The poet himself speaks of feelings that rise from the ashes of loss, burning in the flames of melancholy. He vividly portrays a lingering homesickness for smiles that have departed and the giggles now lamented.

I wish you all the best for keeping up this flavour of writing in poem or prose form of your literary thoughts.

Dr. Vikram Singh,
Literary Laureate and President Prize Awardee.

Endorsements

It is a moment of immense pride and joy for our school as we witness one of our brightest former student Vardaan Vikram Singh, our erstwhile esteemed head boy, take a remarkable step forward with the release of his book. Known for his eloquence and engaging presence, he captivated audience with his natural gift for speaking and impressive dramatic skills. His vibrant personality and extroverted spirit made him a beloved figure among his peers, and his approachable nature allowed him to foster genuine bonds with everyone he met. As a senior, he not only impressed those around him but also set an example of leadership.

His journey reminds us of the impact he has had on our school, both as a student and as a leader and it fills us with great admiration and pride to celebrate his accomplishment today.

Sir Manoj Thomas, Officiating Principal,
St. Paul's Church College
Agra.

I'm writing to express my heartfelt appreciation and admiration for your hard work and dedication on this maiden literary work of yours. As a proud mentor, I can say that students like Vardaan actually bring success and happiness into our lives and inspires us to continue bring the best in them. Vardaan's rhapsodic collection of poems titled Hiraeth is an intense joyride of human emotions of despair, longing, emptiness, bitter sweetness, adoration, ecstasy and nostalgia. Beautifully categorized as Zephyr, Dusk, Eclipse, Elysium and Saudade.

True to its meaning, Hiraeth is the longing of the aspiring poet in Vardaan to take his readers on an unending euphoric journey of myriad feelings interwoven and still yearning for more and more. Let's soak ourselves in this ocean of passions and live the moments crafted by Vardaan for each one of us. Vardaan's Hiraeth shall indeed be a blessing, to his happy readers.

Way to go, blessings always,

Ma'am Sunita Nayar,
St. Paul's Church College

I gaze at the moon and it gazes back at me
For I am the sea, reflecting the memories of the moon
I fill oceans with my bleeding tears
As if each teardrop were a word fallen into these pages
Ruptured from a withered heart, a hiraeth for ages.

I bleed tears and I cry within
For you are the knife I hold too close Too close, to bleed enough.

Zephyr

The Midnight's Concord

'I was in the conquest of the daybreak but it was the night that made me awake'

The Midnight's Concord

Having outdone the greatest of wars
There I was, looking for peace in the world within;
The war that engulfed all my powers
As I lay, left with countless sin.

As I lay in the dead of night
Looking for a shadow in the dark;
Just then hit me something bright
For it was a bluish white spark.

I was immersed in the hues of chilling white
For it was a dark night with a full moon;
The ever so big, looked to sympathize,
Like chunks of hope, in a dim lagoon.

The petals of moonlight that gently fell
On a chaotic surface of a turbulent lake;
As I started my walk along the lonely dell
That led me towards the daybreak.

The miniature spark from the 'immovable force'
That lay unfazed on a lone night sky
Their calm blinks trying hard to end the remorse,
But the bars of my cage were set high.

The lonely dark aura of the night
That brought a silent peace of mind;
The whispery chirp of the crickets,
As if singing a melancholy in the back of my mind.

The calm dew raining gently
As if tears of nature consoling;
The ecstasy of the bats flying swiftly,
The disarming hoots of the owl growling

I looked around, to see all trying to sympathize,
From the bats to the dark sky;
Yet a deserted night for an eye
And yet the dark night trying to pacify.

I was in the conquest of the daybreak
But it was the night that made me awake;
For it wasn't the war outside
It was the war within…

Shadows of Twilight

'That's when the mystics shower Flashing upon the inward eye'

Shadows of Twilight

Drowning in the waters of solitude
There I was, wandering in a pensive mood
Watching the faint moon, as if wrapped in a silk shroud
As I continued to stroll like a lone cloud.

The cirrus clouds that covered the moon
Like a veil covering a bride, in a hot afternoon
As the moon gently scattered faded silver
All over the calm river.

The hues of silver mingled with the whites
That gave both to a faded moonlight
The faint moon lays under the bright Fabrics
of evening sky
As If a young cherub hiding behind her mother, for
being too shy.

It's a bit dark, but it's also blue
The sun's sinking and so there's a tangerine hue
The canvas is all faint with fine strokes
Of light blue and dark paint With faded
moonlight sprinkled
Accompanied by the stars that twinkle.

The calm breeze gently dazzles the flowers
As the river water gushes over the rock scours
There's the cuckoo, and one or two thrushes
That look to take off with the wind that rushes.

There's the gust and rush of water gushing
Painted all over with the evening sky
And there's the sovereign cuckoo's cry
Soon after, faded the occult view
As I left with a final goodbye.

Now when I bestow some veiled beauty with flowers
And yonder upon the sky
That's when the mystics shower
Flashing upon the inward eye.

Woods of Solace

'The lone woods that happily enwraps
As I find peace in its lap. Flashing upon the inward eye'

Woods of Solace

In the deep woods
There lays the mind
For the city lights that keep getting me blind
My eyes are deep and dark
It's been years since I have smiled with an arc.

Those deep shades of the oak
The high-pitched quacks of the toad.
The profound air of the woods that nourishes
And prevents the ache of happiness, the city lights garnish.

The melodies of the cuckoo
That makes my anxiety bid adieu
The mesmerizing smell of the cedar
I wonder if there's a better healer!

It's the friendly nature's room
That makes each of my nerves bloom
The crazy cricket's melancholy
I wonder it's the reason, for the nature's so holy.

The blues of the sky that hail
The miracles of the nature that prevail
The greys of the clouds
That praise the blessings of the nature aloud.
The gentle morning dew that tickles
Each of my veins and tenderly trickles.
The glorious soars of the eagle
It's all a blessing for a man so feeble.

The lone woods that happily enwraps
As I find peace in its lap.
And besides the inner pleasure
There remained utter sadness, for the helpless nature.

Cold Cry

*'Besides the sorrowful winter times Again,
there shall be sunshine!'*

Cold Cry

On the dark days with clouds all around
The dry yellow leaves are not on the ground
For the cool winter breeze gently swirls them
As the winter treats them with contempt.

The large old oak tree is dry
The wild street dogs lay to cry
The cuckoo and its companions have lost their melody
As they beseech the end for winter's cruelty.

The land is in frost
Which has forced the immortal in deep thought
The old chaps budge in shiver
The young lads quiver with fear.

The river water is frozen
Granny's sweaters are the best of the season
The days are the allies
The nights are the foes.

The warm sunny days
The cool night that prevails
The morning melodies of the Robin
The buzz of the flies
It is something where the mind cries.

Besides the sorrowful winter times
Again, there shall be sunshine
When the immortal will again favor a blessing
With the nature again awakening!

The Winter's Tale

'Besides the welcome and farewell And the joys of the Christmas bell.'

The Winter's Tale

In the dark corner of my room
To gaze around the hazy sunshine's fabric loom
As quiet as a star I sat
To cherish the memories of the winter arriving at.

The bustling streets, the occupied men
The children having peanuts every now and then
The women weaving sweaters
For their tiny little toddlers.

The melancholic cry of the frogs
for they bid goodbye
The joyful hurrahs of the boys in denim
For they receive warm welcome

The sayonara of the kingfisher
For they drank the last drop of the summer river
And the melodies of the Siberian crane
For they returned again.

Besides the welcome and farewell
And the joys of the Christmas bell
There remained utter sadness to dwell
For the helpless nature to swell.

Dusk

Memories of Melancholy

*'But is there any brighter day Without a storm of a
rainy washout?'*

Memories of Melancholy

Clouding through the gusts of dejection
Lay above me, the fluffy cottons and dull skies of grey
blue complexion
With the faint blushes of the sun gasping through the
gates of cloudy heavens
As I stuck my head and soul at sixes and sevens.

My hair fluttered with the cool breeze
As I continued to swim in the oceans of mourning seize
I strolled in deserts of solitude, rejection and fear
As glanced upon my cheek was a fragile rain of tear.

The world had abandoned me
Friends neglected me
Home looked like a withered tree
As I had no one to look for
Well of course, except me.

There seemed no roads ahead of me
As the ones behind me vanished in a flee
I was a wandering cloud
Who was nowhere to be found.
My past whispered to me of my glory
As my reality struck a lightning of melancholy.

Just when the magma of my emotions was eloping Fell
upon me, a tear from the gateway of skies
As the cuckoos and Koyal's cried out the goodbyes of
farewell Uprooted trees with withered branches lost their
long-standing legacy

When every head looked for a shade of courtesy.

The strong gusts dethroned the parrots and the pigeons
And assaulted the flowers and leaves
Soon when the sun eclipsed the clouds
The glistening strokes of sunlight fumed through the
misty shroud.

The skies blushed with a pinkish tinge
As the aromas of petrichor sprinkled over the
nature's fringe The greens smiled greener
As the birds echoed sweeter. Tons of them fell,
But thousands of them flourished like heyday;
The greener shrubs smirked and giggled with a fresh
laugh They swayed along with the gusts of nature's craft
As if a cherubin glitters with a wide chuckle
After his mother showers him with soap bubbles.

I wandered for my grief
To escape my way out
But is there any brighter day
Without a storm of a rainy washout?

Nadir

'Just like a mother to her babbling child
As Time Stood and Fate Smiled.'

Nadir

I wandered in the mirages of undying grief
Lost in the labyrinths of despair,
For I stood in all stillness and folly
As blew against me, the winds of melancholy.

Finding myself forgotten in the fields,
Of broken grass and shattered yield
An eternal abyss of nowhere;
Scorched in bygone green and placid fear
With withered trees and wrinkled tear.

I have walked miles, in pitch dark
As I continued ahead, blinded, with no path
I have lost things to find them
Cocooned in the shadows of darkness
And enwrapped in the solemn skies of stillness.

Drowned in the oceans of fragmented glee
It was my eye that bleed the sea
I looked around for shores, but there were none to see
As everything drifted along, as if an aimless boat
deserted at sea.

But destiny doth harbour wrecked boats
For it embraces and clasps
Just like a mother to her babbling child
As Time Stood and Fate Smiled.

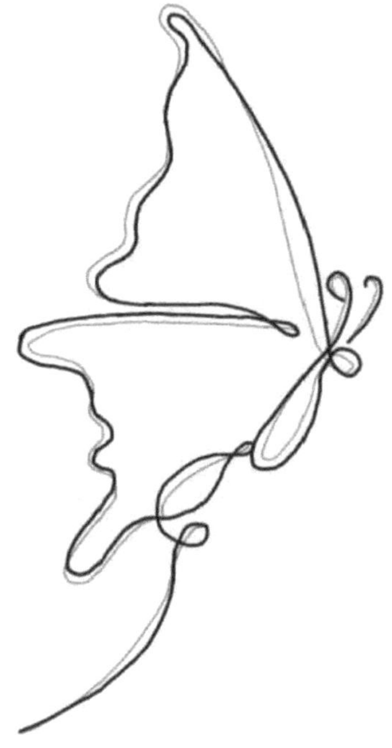

I live, but what for?

'*Which makes me wonder, I live, but what for?*'

I live, but what for?

————————— ✦ ◆ ✦ —————————

I dwell in the gusts of life
Without the zephyrs of living.
I breathe in the airs of survival
Leaving behind the hoping breeze of revival.
I breathe, but what for?
I survive, but I don't exist anymore.

For once I was the essence of your living
Now the witness to my own death
As I no more gasp for any breath
I walk in the shadows of the past
Only to find a graveyard of the memories, that passed.

I have plucked myself and fallen
Like wrinkled leaves in autumn
Like the night owl hoots and releases a new album;
When the silence creeps and shadows prevail
When the graveyards mutter and epitaphs smile
When laughter cries on its coffin's exile.

I live but what for?
I smile and cheer but what for?
I giggle with tear but what for?
I scream and cry out but what for?
I whisper my melancholy

But what for?

I drift away, sailing
In the aimless waters of despair
I now choke in vacant air
For I have crumbled in this war
Which makes me wonder,
I live, but what for?

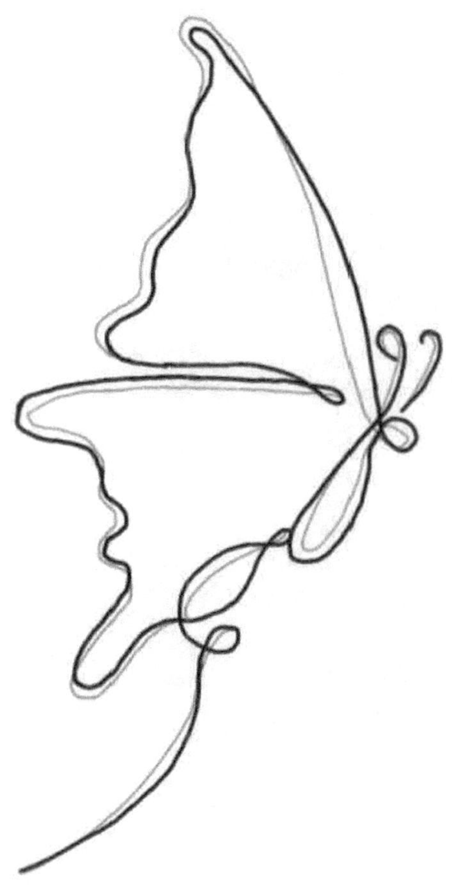

Winds of Sorrow

'They left my soul's ash warm
To bring me peace, after the storm.'

Winds of Sorrow

There I woke under the fine hues
Of the cotton candy blues
In the frosting breezes of melancholy
Which looked ever so holy.

The flawless glories of the cuckoo
That looked ever so elegant
Aah, the auroras of the morning blue
On the fabrics of the sky avenue.

The Sun that lay hid
In the skies, oh so turbid
As the flowers that grooved gently
On the beats of the morning indie.

There was I in the most pleasant
Zion That ever so gently absorbed me
Drowned in the winds of melancholy,
Far away from any jolly.

But I stood still
Amidst the winds of melancholy
Maybe I had a bit more than my capacity
Frozen by the frosting gusts

Until my cold sweat turned to rust.
It was inevitable of the storm
To come to a halt
But it was all on me To bear the assault.
It was a cold tempest Got my
Trunks ripped But not my will
For at least the day, I die until.

The violent winds that blew
As they pierced my heart through
They left my soul's ash warm
To bring me peace, after the storm.

Invincible

'But me, who was the captain of my soul
The master of my fate.'

Invincible

In the dark clouds
My heart and soul speaking aloud
There you may retreat
Or further you may regret.

For the devil in front of me
The past smiling kindly
For one mistake and everything is gone
There will be every reason to mourn.

Like an injured bird
In the howling nights waiting patiently
As I held back kindly
It was all on me to decide my destiny.

I realized I was in the dark times
Like a bird stuck in the charcoal mines
Like a frightened snake in a mole
There I was, at the fault of my soul.

Losing all hope
The Sun again shone
Screeching through darkness to allocate
Instructing myself that it was no one,
But me, who was the captain of my soul
The master of my fate.

Eclipse

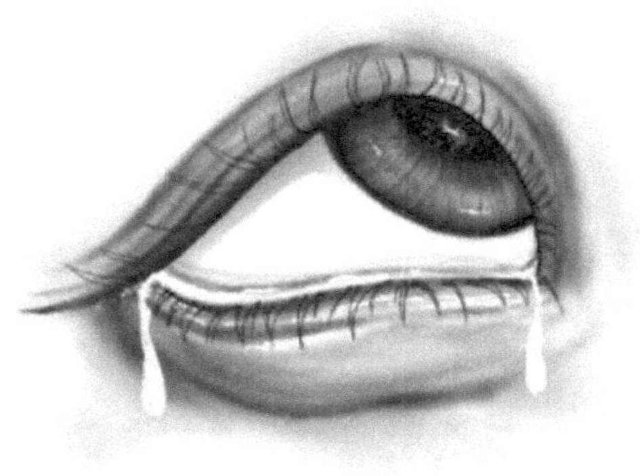

Unshed Tears

'Once they laughed at me Now I laugh at them!!'

Unshed Tears

✦ ◆ ✦

There I was in the darkness
Happily allowing my tears to pass
With no one to stand by
For the hopes I lost in the grass

The heart was broken
The mind was without fear
For I had gone through the worst
They weren't stopping
for they were my tears.

Just sitting in the dark corners
With no one to share the past
Allowing my days to pass by
For I thought I wasn't going to last

My heart and soul started to fade
There was no sympathy of shade
My feelings, my hope, my belief flew away
Like the particles of ashes.

I was once the iron
But now I have turned to rust
For they showed no pity in the long run
Everyone left me to disintegrate in the dust.

For though the world laughed at me But I laughed too

For they couldn't see my heart and soul crying too.

I made the kids smile
For they couldn't bare to see me cry
I allowed the people to laugh
As I had no other hopes for miles.

It was the time to wake from ash and dust
As I wiped my tears and rust
Though it was a journey to walk alone
With no one to trust on
Yet it was the time to walk on.

I mended my heart and soul
There were no longer fake smiles
I walked away from hoax sympathies
For they were no longer my companions for miles.

I walked and walked
On my way to decide destiny
As I neglected the past as a dream
It was all on me, whom I could believe.

I turned from a day dreamer to a self-BELIEVER
Everyone believed I couldn't make it without help Once
they laughed at me
Now I laugh at them!!

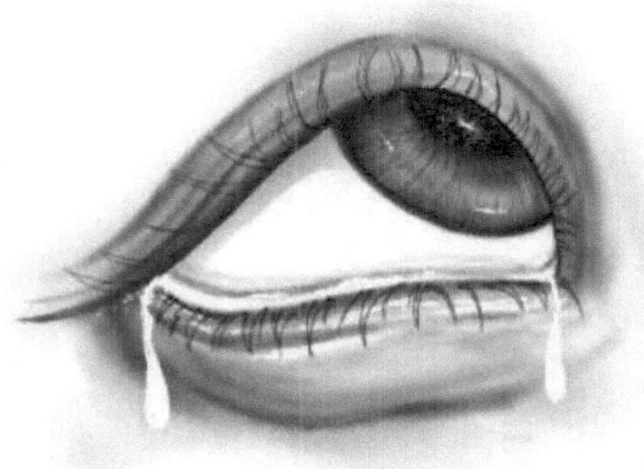

Banshees of Hatred

*'Still couldn't figure out the hate Wasn't
I the creature from the same blood?'*

Banshees of Hatred

My mind was with fear
For it was surrounded by hatred
Though without a guilt of mine
My soul was dipped in tears.

I was being bullied
For I was night like dark
Still no fault revealed
As there was no hope of a spark.

They would troll me For I was fat
For I was a peasant's son
With no money to even buy a hat.

I was surrounded by hatred
For I belonged to another race
For the divisions they created
Love and support had no place.

My soul was left alone
My mind had turned to stone
With no one there for a shoulder
To keep my head crying on.

For I never realized
The human race has hatred for its own fellow mate

There's only enmity and dislike in this flood Still couldn't
figure out the hate
Wasn't I the creature from the same blood?

Long Walk To Freedom

'Now they call me a revolutionary
Leader That's my Long Walk to Freedom!'

Long Walk To Freedom

There I started alone
Among the farmers and the houses of clay
From happy chirping masses
With no bed to Lay.

Exploitation was the only preach
Amidst the crisis and poverty
As the difficulties I screeched Now
I fight for poverty.

For I was the coal in the ice
They believed I was inadequate
For they were sure I was not fit to be the President
As I was not a regular resident.

I rose like truth In the land of lies
Like a light shining
In the deep darkness.

I stood high among the masses
Where my friends, my people
Were thought to be ashes
Then I led them to fire!

Now they call me the 'Madiba'
For I became the President of
South Africa I perished the slavery of my people

And drove away the 'Ice.'
Now they call me a revolutionary
Leader That's my Long Walk to Freedom!

Changes

'The world is my cage,
She came, for I required a change.'

Changes

— ✦ ◆ ✦ —

She set foot in my life
For I required a change
When the waters of my foppery
Had outpoured, and my sins outcasted
She came for I required a change.

When destiny adored me
You arrived,
Like that of the rustling wind
That gathers and carries along with it,
Every fallen leaf,
Withered and broken from its tree
As I followed the wings of your wind
When you took off, in a flee.

An exasperated and dusted midnight traveler
Travelling through his ways
From thick and thin, To storm and wind,
When shone upon me,
The enshrining light of your presence
When every wound, every tear
Restored and glistened to its flair.

You were the wind to my wings
The light to my days
Now I just flutter in dry nights
The world is my cage,
She came, for I required a change.

A Sky Full of Stars

*'A Sky full of Stars,
A Soul full of hidden potential'*

A Sky Full of Stars

A Sky full of Stars,
A Soul full of hidden potential
Often does the clouds conceal the stars yet
they are never lost,
But always there, waiting to be found....

You look up to the Sky to find it embedded with Stars
You look within and you find yourself decorated with
powers The clouds of failure try to hide them
But can't demolish the natural existence
All you need is to find them within
Those Powers of Resistance that stopped you from going
the wrong way That Capability with which
you won your very first battle
That Capacity of hope that kept you alive in the
Gloomiest of times

And that Will of Desire that always kept you alive!
These are those stars, no one can snatch from you (not
even your gloomy days) Look within and you shall
retrieve your greatest present that always laid within you

Elysium

Khil Khilata Chand

*'Your smile makes most of my day and why not?
You have the arc smile of the crescent moon'*

Khil khilata Chand
(Giggling Moon)

I have walked miles in the labyrinths
Of strange and serene pits of misery
And when I was in the deepest trench of despair
Shone upon me the light ray of a morning fair.

The birth of a warmth within
And rise of waters of jolly
Breathing through the columns of my heart
And aching every inch of my chest so far.

It's the hazy Sunkissed brown morning hues
Of your fluttering hair Dancing and blooming with each
Surpassing winds of breeze of heaven.
The eerie's of the blowing air
Gently talking to your hair
As they groove in the windy Days
As they dance and bounce
Just like the ping pong walls of my heart.

That's when I gaze into the microcosmic
Nebulas like bulging eyes of yours
Brown like sun scorched autumn leaves
And prettier grey than a cloud hit moon

I see the gaseous nebulas and moon in your eyes
And probably even the moon has flaw spots
But none in your eyes Your pretty stunted nose
And those red velvet lips of yours

Pretty enough to boil, evaporate and melt every heart
wall of mine The falling restless eyes of yours
Remind me of falling in those trenches of beauty.
I see blue waves of the sea and the blue
Canvas of the sunlit skies
And all do lead me to the mysteries
Of care, warmth and love in your eyes.

Your smile makes most of my day and why not?
You have the arc smile of the crescent moon
Each time you giggle and smile
I have found in you The sweetest naïve kid
That I wish to always to take care of and pamper.

You have had your bad days And I have had mine
But just wipe off your tears
Cause I am here to stay and we'll just be fine.
Didduu

Falling In Spring

'It was spring and now it came to a standstill
And so did you.'

Falling In Spring

When the tranquil sun glistened its warmth over the
shores of your face Your eyes shone like
those of a new born cherub
And that little hair strand glanced its groove over your
gentle eyes When the gusts of wind blew over to you.

Spring was in its bloom And so were you
The daisies and the pansies were fluttering with ecstasy
And so were your joyous arms as you danced and
grooved like a sunlit sunflower at dawn
Your smile would remind me of dawn
The blues the whites the tangerines
All filled into a drop that would light up the skies
Is this the start of something wonderful and new?
Or one more dream that I cannot make true?

The endless depth of your wandering eyes
calling for the dreamy seas of adore
As I looked to drown myself in those
When the cotton candy smudged lips would remind me
of a moonlit garden filled with auroras of the city of stars
and drizzling sleepy flowers.

It was spring
And the sun scorched leaves We're falling for the breeze
And so was I for those glazing eyes and dancing
blooming hair.

And perhaps fate adored you more
It was spring and now it came to a standstill
And so did you.

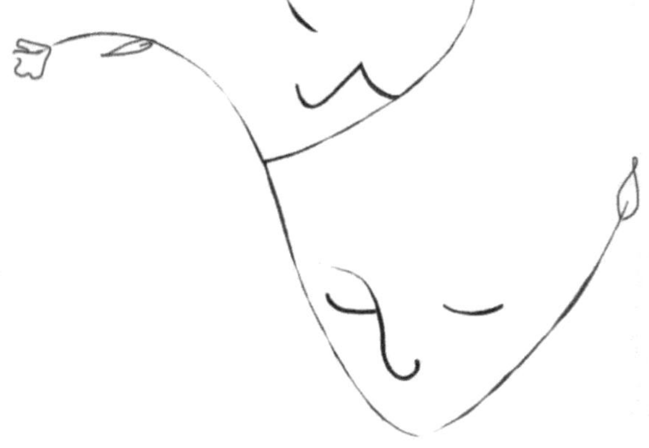

Music to the Muse

'I urge to drown in your large cherubin like eyes The dark luscious sea like eyes of yours'

Music to the Muse

With each sunrise as the serene sunlight
Hits the sails of my heart
Each depth of my heart aches for those
gentle eyes of yours
With each grain of my mind longing
for that succulent giggle of yours.

As the turbulent gust of heaven weaver
The fabrics of your stranded hair
The sun-soaked raven hair tied back in pink ends
As each time, my longing and adoration transcends.

I urge to drown in your large cherubin like eyes
The dark luscious sea like eyes of yours
Make me fall
Each time like falling leaves in autumn
The way you straight fell from heaven
Each time I glance over my eyes on you
Your eyes are a dessert
As each time my heart longs for you like a winter bird.

The burnt scars you embrace on your right hand
Bring oceans of melancholy to my soul.
I shine each time like a sunlit sailing top
Honey, we have spent quite some best weeks
And I don't want to stop.

Inception

*'You are the hope that crackles
Like a flittering flame, making every storm fickle.'*

Inception

When the glaciers of night
Melt by the outcasts of a glimmering glance of the sun
Reminds me of the glistened sun
Shining ever so gently on your face.

When the sun peeps through the darkness
Of the night, with the beams of sparkling vile
Brightening up the vacant night
So do you, with your infectious smile.
You are the hope that crackles
Like a flittering flame, making every storm fickle.

Tangled like Rapunzel, and uncursed
By the gentle morning gust that sways
And unfurls you're not so 'blonde' hair;
As if they preach poetry to the skies and cloudy haze.

As if you are the muse to the birth of day
Like a new Dawn,
Bringing smiles slowly as you make your way
As if you resonate with the symphonies
Of the early cuckoo Makes me wonder
If not you, then who?

Like a crack of dawn
Giving birth to each life and day
Arousing ecstasy and euphoria
Like the birds that twitter
And early cow and their calves that moo
My inward eye flutters,
That the crack of dawn is none other than you!

Light

*'You may be in Darkness
but the Light within you, isn't.'*

Light

It's all Darkness, isn't it?
A luminous world
But every light you see,
Leaves impressions of Darkness and that Light?
that Light is itself a shadow of darkness

You are walking in those depths of darkness
where it's all pitch dark
but when you glare in an empty void
You can sense the tiniest spark of the light that you look
for You try to walk, but it's all dark
You look around, the dark haunts you back
But there's still that one pinch of hope that's left behind

Your Eyes Maybe Dim
But Your Soul isn't
You may be in Darkness
but the Light within you, isn't........

Saudade

The story of my life

'Death is all we wait
And forever happiness remains a bait'

The Story of My Life

Within the trenches of my veins lies stories untold
And every page waiting to be unfolded
With Every beating pulse weaving a new story
Waiting to sing its echoes of melancholy.

These courtyards cry out my running footsteps
Terraces are an exhibition to my ecstasy for cricket
As these walls have spectated
My days of hope, loss and glory
As every corner is a mirror to a new story.

Swaying and swinging on this wind
And a weary course to sleep under my grandma's skin
Wondering in the orchids of fairies
With no worry or excuse
Lying in her lap for a motherly truce.

These lakes are a stream to my morning zest
And this house?
A museum of screams, lullabies and cries to my guests.

When I was conferred to the heights
I fell harder than the skies
And when I was abandoned and left
I smiled harder with my chest.

When I would fail,
I would look at the skies and the cloudy veil.
And when my love lost,
I had won but at what cost?

Probably I was too late
For we all live up to fate
Death is all we wait
And forever happiness remains a bait.

Hiraeth

'I stop and smile at my destiny's sweet rebel As I shake hands, with the devil.'

Hiraeth

In evenfall's sigh, when silhouettes play
An ache arouses, at the heart's bay
Hiraeth whispers in my ear, the ache of absence
As it Echoes aloud my every sin.

I long for the days, that died
And now a happy smile is a shroud
On a teary man's melancholic face that he vowed;
A scent of looks and a look of fate's ugly tide
In my heart's Adobe, that is where memories reside.

In dreams, I see the ghosts of love
Ashes of what could never rise above
Shadows of my past giggling in the dark
As I stare at it, from a bruised mark.

And yet I grip hold of it
I wear myself in its every fit.
For in its essence, I find solace true
A comfort that sees me through.

My hiraeth whispers its sighs
When I look at myself a chuckling child,
I stop and smile at my destiny's sweet rebel
As I shake hands, with the devil.

Saudade

*'I told the stars about you
How you were a giggling, rose kissed by morning dew'*

Saudade

I told the stars about you
How you were a giggling, rose kissed by morning dew,
Like a bathing daffodil,
Dancing in the sunny hues.

I talked to the moon about you
How you could melt the moonlight out of the starry
night's blue Like your eyes always did,
Melting the sparkles off my heart's lid.

You are the mirror I would stare at for hours Only if I
could find you in me
And scent your secrets in your hair
Wish I could again write your name, with my tear.

Scarred Demons

'The demons you hide, and the secrets you enclose
I stand and see a river of suppressed tears that flows.'

Scarred Demons

The bruised skin on your hand
The blemished blood over it
As if time froze, and so did the blood
As if storms poured, and air stopped.

The black blue cracks
The swollen plasma around
Are the mirrors,
To the pain and brawl
That you have carried throughout.

I wander within you
Among the scars and bruises
The demons you hide, and the secrets you enclose
I stand and see a river of suppressed tears that flows.

And within thee, I found a strength
That held onto every scar of yours
That carries within, a new dawn
Of a war, yet to be won.

Unbroken

'You are the Essence to the Deepest of your lies.
You are the Soul to the very own process of healing'

Unbroken

How far you have travelled
With all the storms
Trying to sink you
But you have surpassed them all.
You have fought well
In the moments
You thought you never could.
Appreciate your efforts
Cause you have been outstanding in the
worst of the situations.
Embrace yourself and carry on with your efforts.

In the toughest and outrageous of storms,
You have come out with utmost determination
You have come out of the times
You never thought you could.
So why to fear of the future storms?
Will your struggling efforts be ever depreciated?
Will your value be ever decreased?
Your fighting spirit shall forever remain
the same till eternity.
You have gone through a lot
In all those times, You even broke down
You had no hope

And there was always that one spirit,
which was struggling, within you
And that spirit was yours.

You absorbed all those humiliations
You accepted all those scars
You still kept on with the hustle
And that's the authentic spirit of yours
And those scars, you carry within
Are the symbol of what you have been through
And most importantly a mark of your
never dying spirit in all times.
The deepest Essence lies in you.
You are the captain of your soul.
You are the master of your fate.
You are yourself. Your Essence for healing lies in you.
You are the answer to all of your worries.

You are the essence to all of your worries
You are the essence to all of your struggles.
You are the essence to the deepest of your Scars.
You are the Essence to the Deepest of your lies.
You are the Soul to the very own process of healing.

The woods are lovely, dark and deep,
but I have promises to keep,
and miles to go before I sleep,
and miles to go before I sleep.

Robert Frost

Epilogue

Dear passerby,

Amidst the tides and halts of life, nebulas of chaos surround our gentle, placid stream of life. We often find ourselves drenched in a havoc of complications and problems. While people fade and bonds blur, what eternalizes the essence of life, are the epitaph memories of the people we lost and the moments we live. How living people die and how flourishing moments vanish.

While sometimes we forever want to cling onto our past, our destinies may force us to erase their existence. When some moments that we deeply cherish, become the reasons for our melancholy. When our most beautiful dreams, mould themselves to a haunting nightmare. When we once gaze at our future under the shadows of the moon and now we stare empty at it, reflecting reminiscences of our past. When the people, the things, we once loved the most, fade into blurring memories echoing melancholy.

Our Shadows from the past whisper dejection, that's when we long for those moments, memories and time. The memories we lost like trifling sand grains in an hourglass.

This longing is a mirror to our reflections, and the time we lost in the past. When fate played its cards and this time, this period of euphoria forever seizes. When time stops, and fate smiles.

I hope each poem in this book reminded you of a road you took or a path you lost.

May Hiraeth stay with you, a gentle reminder of life's eternal giggling miseries and sobbing happiness

Sincerely,
Vardaan Vikram Singh

About The Author

In evenfall's sigh, gleams a hiraeth. When silhouettes of the past bloom in the shadows, a longing, a yearning awaits. Sitting on the shores of melancholy, staring at the empty skies of longing, Vardaan cries his heart and spills his tears in the magical words of these pages. Too trifle for his age, and too old for his yearning, Vardaan Vikram Singh is a 19 year old writer, poet, film fiction and theatre enthusiast, smoked admirer of music with a degree in classical music, an active follower of chess and a rookie martial art and cricket player, and ironically enough, an inquisitive physics devotee. A former student and head boy from St. Pauls, a Harvard accepted and currently pursuing engineering from Delhi.

Growing up, running and hustling from the Taj-estic streets of Agra, Vardaan found Solace in the intriguing ways of life at a very young age of 15. Descending from a family of writers and scholars, Vardaan looked up to his father to draw his inspiration.

Initially, intrigued and rooted by Nature, Vardaan began with writing nature imageries. Each nature imagery echoing a tale of sympathy to the dejected and lost.Gradually, with the flows of time, he explored other themes of love, loss and nostalgia.

Each poem in the collection has seen a different shade in Vardaan' s life. Fueled by personal experiences and perceptions, Vardaan has tried to bring a new life to his soliloquies of homesickness for a home that never was.

Contact number: 8445733028
Email: vvs7believer@gmail.com
Or insta handle :- @v._ v._.s

www.ingramcontent.com/pod-product-compliance
Lightning Source LLC
Chambersburg PA
CBHW031259130726
47988CB00007B/2643